SEO

WHITE BOOK

THE ORGANIC GUIDE TO GOOGLE
SEARCH ENGINE OPTIMIZATION

R.L. Adams

ISBN-10: 1484815084
ISBN-13: 978-1484815083

R.L. ADAMS

All Rights Reserved

FTC & Legal Notices

CONTENTS

WHAT IS SEO?

SEO is search engine optimization. It is the set of methods and techniques used for increasing the Website ranking for a listing on a search engine's results pages.

SEO involves some basic principles that when practiced and applied correctly, and over an extended period of time, will result in very noticeable positive increases to a Website's rankings.

But we all know it's not as simple as that right?

True, unless you have the right guide that offers not only a clear overview of how the process works, but also provides some direct practical methods for improving your Website's visibility.

This is that guide.

Depending on how new you are to the SEO industry, you need to be aware of the changes that have occurred.

Google has evolved and its algorithm has been beefed up.

What does this even mean?

Well, without the proper knowledge of just how to conduct your SEO tasks you may accidentally become the target of some of the defense systems that Google has erected in the wake of these changes it's made.

If you're going to succeed with SEO you need to know the new rules of the Web; Google's new rules. I'm talking about Google here, because, let's face it, Google is king of the Web. It always has been and it most likely always will be.

The Google search engine wields a clear dominance over its rivals with 83% of all search engine traffic coming from the search giant, according to *The Pew Research Center's Internet & American Life Project 2012 Tracking Survey.* That's a huge dominance. Huge.

So, why exactly did Google change its rules?

Google's been screwed over. It really has been. There was a silent war being waged in the depths of Cyberspace behind the scenes that saw Google's grip on the Internet slowly slipping away and into the hands of an elite group of SEO specialists who reigned supreme on the Web.

This elite group could control nearly any Google Search Engine Search Results Page (or SERP), making their own multiple listings appear at the top quickly and effectively. In turn this elite group dominated Google's SERPs and wielded free reign over any industry or niche they chose to churn a profit in.

Google needed to take back the Internet so it did what any multibillion dollar Multinational Corporation would do: it changed the rules.

Google had to fight back. It had no choice. It took its own search engine algorithm and it spun it on top of its head introducing three major updates that completely obliterated the search engine landscape, as we know it; this was Google's atomic bomb.

The long time professional SEO elite group of "manipulators" was left scratching their heads in the wake of the massive blast radius that shook the Internet by storm. Now, this may sound a bit farfetched or exaggerated to you, but I assure you it's not.

Why is this important for you to know?

Well, if you're just coming into SEO or you're relatively new, you need to make sure that you approach your optimization with care. You have to handle it with kid gloves. Because there's so much information out there that is now actually misinformation, and if you try to use some of the tactics discussed by many articles and books on the Web that were published prior to these massive rule changes, you may end up accidently hurting your Website's ranking as opposed to helping it. Now that's not good at all, is it?

I'm here to help you uncover and unravel all of the mystery behind these fabled attacks that took the Internet by storm and I'm here to deconstruct how to do SEO today, with tact and care that will lead to long term SERP improvements for any Website.

WHO THIS BOOK IS FOR

This book is for anyone who's just starting out in the SEO field that has a basic understanding of what SEO is. If you are brand new to the field, this book will help you deconstruct and understand the complicated world of SEO. If you're looking for an even more basic primer to SEO, you can also check out the second book in this series entitled *SEO Simplified – Learn Search Engine Optimization Strategies and Principles for Beginners*, available online at Amazon.

If you've been involved with SEO or have had some experience with it, and you're frustrated with not being able to find a complete, easy to read guide to just how the industry works then this book is for you.

What I've come to notice in the SEO industry is one of two things:

SEO Books are either outdated, don't provide enough information, and don't provide complete information.

SEO Books provide too much theory and not enough real usable methods for improving search results rankings.

This book is entitled SEO White Book. Why? The title refers to something called White-Hat SEO, a term used within the SEO field to refer to acceptable SEO practices that adhere to Google's Webmaster Guidelines.

White-Hat SEO exists in retrospect to Black-Hat SEO, which involve a bit more grey-area type SEO tactics that was the topic of one of my last books entitled, *The SEO Black Book – A Guide to the Industry's Secrets*. Although that book isn't specifically about Black-Hat SEO itself, some of the techniques in the book can be considered to be Black-Hat SEO techniques if they are not applied exactly in the way recommended.

So, whether you're new to SEO, or you've had some experience with it, this book will shed light on the new Google SEO rules that are now dominating the search engine landscape. By reading and understanding this new set of rules you will have the firepower to go out and conduct SEO work the right way that will help you rank higher and faster in the long run, without potentially harming your Website by breaking the rules.

1

EARNING GOOGLE'S TRUST

The name of the game today is trust. More specifically, earning Google's trust. To earn its trust today you need to prove yourself. Gone are the days when this just occurred automatically by registering a domain name and slapping together a Website.

Today, Google's trust not only has to be earned, but it has to be earned over time. It won't happen quickly. Why does this matter? Because this one single concept is going to affect everything that you do when it comes to SEO in a post Google Panda and Penguin world.

Google Panda and Penguin?

The Google Panda and Google Penguin were algorithm changes that occurred to the search giant's formulas for ranking. These were devastating. In fact, these two changes were the atomic bomb of the industry. The new rules left a wake of casualties in the form of Websites that lost huge amounts of rankings and some that completely fell off of Google's indexes all together. This was considered by some, death by Google.

Why did this happen?

An elite group of SEO specialists had formed that really began to take advantage of their knowledge in the field. They knew precisely how to manipulate a Website to reach the top of Google's search engine results pages (SERPs) and in turn make a killing peddling just about anything they wanted to. No matter what search term it was, their elite specialized knowledge could get them to the top, fast, for virtually any search. It was a huge upper hand.

Panda Attacks

Google had to respond and it did in a major way. It launched the Google Panda first back in February of 2011. The Google Panda went into this "Panda Attack" mode and it went out looking for all the Websites that had low quality content with poor user experience. It found these Websites and karate chopped the listings down the rankings, some of them almost entirely off its indexes altogether.

Websites that were hit hard were the content farms and link farms. Yes, they were called farms, and just like farms that grow crops in the real world, these virtual farms were a hotbed for low quality content that was spun in a hundred different ways just for the purpose of building more links back to the main page using primary keywords.

Similarly, link farms were sites that housed articles with an excessive number of links off the page. The articles themselves were decent but the purpose of the article was to link out to many different sites. You see, when the Google spider gets to a page, the way that it finds the rest of the Internet is by following links. These sites had thousands of links to various other Websites over the span of few articles and pages. These sites were karate-chopped down as well.

Google has launched more than two-dozen of these Panda attacks since the first one reared its head back in February of 2011. The Panda attacks have been major but they haven't been as severe as the Google Penguin attacks. The Penguin attacks were much more geared towards this elite group of SEO specialists who bended and broke Google's rules.

Penguin Attacks

The Penguin attacks were launched in April of 2012 and it targeted these sites that were propelled to the top of rankings by techniques that violated Google's Webmaster Guidelines severely. These were more of the sites that participated in things like keyword stuffing, content cloaking, and created elaborate low quality link schemes that included both link pyramids and link wheels.

These Penguin attacks were devastating. They offered a major blow to the SEO industry that had once prided itself on being able to implement certain techniques to propel sites to the top of Google's SERPs. Not anymore.

EMD Attacks

There was also one other major algorithm change that first launched in September of 2012, announced by

Google's own head of Webspam, Matthew Cutts. Google went after low quality exact-match domains (EMDs) that were targeting keyword searches.

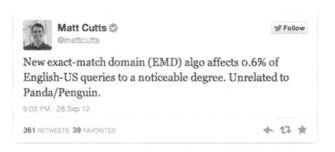

What's an EMD?

An exact-match domain, or EMD for short, is a domain name that is registered to target a specific keyword. For example, if you were doing a website on iPhone 6 Rumors, an EMD would be iPhone6Rumors.com. Again, this same group of SEO elite specialists used their knowledge of EMDs to target popular keyword searches, and it worked for a while.

Today, an EMD will still work, but it needs to be a high quality EMD. It can't be a low quality one that is registered and propped up with poor content and a bad user experience. If the EMD is high quality with a diverse group of authority links it will still work, however, in most of the cases, people were propping up low quality EMDs just to target certain searches. That's all but over now.

EARNING GOOGLE'S TRUST

Today, to rank high, Google needs to trust you. After getting burned for so long, the new rules have created an entirely new breed of SEO elite operatives who's goal it is to get to the top of Google's search results again. But this time things are different.

This new elite SEO group understands Google's new rules and what it's asking for. They know it is going to take a lot more work for them to get Website's to the top of SERPs again so they have their work cut out for them. They've realized that a top ranked listing today must have the following:

1. Trust through age

2. Trust through authority

3. Trust through content

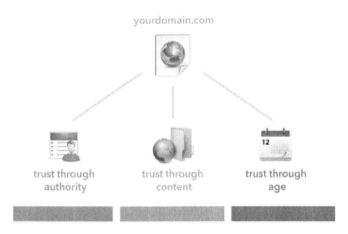

TRUST THROUGH AGE

For Google to trust you today, the first of the three components required for a top ranking listing is trust through age. What does this mean? It means that you must have what's called an aged domain name. An aged domain name is a domain that has been around for 2 years or more. This doesn't mean you registered it two years ago. It means that Google must have found it and indexed it at some point at least 2 or more years ago.

Don't have an aged domain?

If you don't have an aged domain, and you're stuck with a brand new domain, you have some work ahead of you. In my book entitled *The SEO Black Book – A Guide to the Industry's Secrets* I discuss just how to go about allocating an aged domain name. But, since this may be considered by some to be a Black-Hat SEO technique it is not

19

included in the content of this book.

The work that you have ahead of you when your domain is not aged is a very difficult one. If you have the time on your hands, you should be okay to make some significant strides in SERP improvements. However, if you don't have the time, this will be incredibly more difficult.

Google trusts an aged domain because it knows that this Website has been around for a long time. Because of that, it's instantly more trusted than a brand new domain that has just come out in the clear pursuit of top Google SERP rankings. The search engine knows all the tricks now. At one point, the old SEO elite group could register brand new domain name and within a short week or two get to the top of Google's SERPs. Not anymore.

TRUST THROUGH AUTHORITY

Authority is created on the Internet by getting other Websites that Google already trusts to link back to your Website. To do this, you need very high PageRank Websites creating links back to your own Website.

What's PageRank? It's the overall rank – out of a highest possible number of 10 and a lowest possible number of 0 – of a Webpage on the Internet. PageRank is determined by traffic volume so Websites like Facebook, Google, and YouTube all have very high PageRanks, and other Websites with little traffic can have little to no PageRank.

What's important here for authority is that the Website has a lot of different links from not only high PageRank Websites, but everything in between as well. Besides for that, the links have to be organic as well. They can't look like they've been generated by automated link building software, especially if all the links look exactly the same and don't look organic.

This is evident to Google if for example, you go out and generate thousands of links to your Website all with the same keyword in a very short period of time. Google will know you're trying to cheat. This is what the Google Penguin went after; these are the so-called "link schemes".

In my other book, *The SEO Black Book – A Guide to the Industry's Secrets*, I discuss going out and purchasing a high volume set of links, however, I also discuss feeding these links to Google very slowly on a gradual basis, making them appear much more organic. However, since this is a purely White-Hat SEO book, I don't recommend this technique unless you are looking to try a slightly more risky approach.

TRUST THROUGH CONTENT

Building trust through content means that you have to create Webpages or articles that have high quality well researched content that is unique. You can't just slap together page for a text and expect it to rank well. Not only must the underlying content be good, it must be written and optimized from an SEO perspective.

What does this mean? The content has to be keyword rich with your primary keyword and must follow a certain set of rules (to be discussed) in order for the content to rank high. If you have these two points addressed, you will be able to build trust through content.

This is not easy, however, and building trust through content takes time. In fact, it must happen over time for Google to trust it more. If you attempt to push out 10 "okay" articles per day and SEO them to all heck, it won't provide you with as much "SEO juice" as you would get by writing one excellent piece of Web content that is well written, well researched, unique, and superbly optimized for SEO, every other day.

WHERE DO WE GO FROM HERE?

While this may seem like a lot of information and a lot of areas to address, but the more you get acclimated to building SEO-driven content, the easier it will get for you. In the pages to follow, I will discuss how you can take steps, today, to address each of the three main components to optimize your Webpage for SEO.

One thing that's important for you to keep in mind, however, is that SEO takes time. It's not going to happen overnight. While there are cases of seeing quick results, if you have a fairly new domain name, that doesn't have a lot of authority, expect to allow several months to go by before you start seeing considerable results.

Yes, I know it's frustrating, but these are the safeguards that Google has put in place. However, once your domain name becomes trusted, any content that you post will move to the top of search results much faster and you won't have to wait months. This is why you see certain pieces of content from some news Websites like Mashable, TechCrunch, and Huffington Post that target a specific keyword at the top of Google search results at times. It's because Google already trusts those sites a great deal and they have spent years building strong authority.

2

BUILDING TRUST THROUGH AGE

After the digital dust settled from the World Wide Web War that Google waged silently in Cyberspace, it created a virtual sandbox where Website's would go if they either misbehaved or were new. This virtual sandbox is called the *Google Sandbox* or the *Sandbox Effect*.

If you end up breaking Google's rules, or you have a new Website, you are placed in Google's Sandbox. When you're in Google's Sandbox, no matter what online efforts you partake in related to the SEO of your Webpage its effects will be filtered through the Sandbox. This means that links won't count as much, content won't rank as high, and so on.

Many new Website owners have experienced this without even knowing it. Many newcomers to the Web that register brand new domains and try to use every SEO trick in the book are hit with the Google Sandbox. They may see their listing climbing at first, but then watch it drop like a hawk swooping in for its prey. It's a dismal drop to the digital bottom of Google's SERPs but it happens every minute of every day.

This is where knowing what you're doing is critical when it comes to SEO. Aside from having a new domain name, your chances are still much better than if you try to force the SEO of your Website and Google flags it as participating in link schemes, keyword stuffing, or any of the other now highly volatile practices of Black-Hat SEO. If you don't know what you're doing, you could get burned badly.

Even if you end up hiring a professional, if they don't know what they're doing, they could end up hurting your domain name, even if you've been around for more than 2 years. When this happens Google punishes you by placing you into its Sandbox, even if the domain name is more than 2 years old.

How do I know all this?

Well, aside from being well versed in the field of SEO, I have tested and tried just about every single technique in the book since the catastrophic Google Penguin and Google Panda attacks. I've tried these on new domains, old domains, and everything in between. I know what works and what doesn't and in *The SEO Black Book – A Guide to the Industry's Secrets* I discuss some of the more risky techniques, but since rules can change at any time, it's really a decision that a Website owner has to make on their own of which direction they want to pursue.

If you're the type that likes to play it safe, then the most organic and natural approach is the best way for you to do this. You can never beat the organic approach, no matter how hard you try to automate things. For some, you may end up saving yourself some time in the beginning, but that factor may be cut short if Google finds you in violation of its rules and karate chops you down the SERPs.

You can never mimic exactly an organic approach with automated link building, period. You can come close, but there's nothing like having a real human being doing the link building for you. However, for some people who simply don't have the time to go out there and build hundreds or even thousands of links they opt for the easier route.

The purely White-Hat SEO approach involves building trust through age over time, no matter what you're doing, it has to be organic. As a long-term strategy, this is probably the best bet, however, some people simply don't want to wait around for months or years to hit the top of Google's SERPs. They want it to happen now.

In order to build that trust through age with Google, you need to address two main key factors as it relates to your Webpages. These two main factors are as follows:

1. The age of your domain name.

2. The age of your content.

The Age of your Domain Name

If you are lucky enough to have an older domain name that you simply haven't done too much work with, but had been indexed by Google two or more years ago, then you're in luck. If you have a brand new, or slightly new domain name, then you have your work cut out for you.

Why does the age matter so much?

Imagine going to the bank to ask for a loan for a new business that you just started, or for one that is fairly new. Everyone knows that in most instances, banks are very hesitant to provide you with a loan for a business like this because it has no history. The bank has no idea what will happen to the business, and in fact, statics show that in most cases more than half of these new business will go belly-up.

Think of Google as the bank. It's not going to give out top listing search results to just anyone, especially to new domain names. Google wants to see you build trust through age. Of course, this is difficult because you can't force time to move any faster than it does, but there are some ways that you can quicken the pace of trust through age by focusing more of your efforts on the other components involved with rank such as authority and content.

The Age of your Content

As you build content on the Web and release it out into the world, it begins to age. Of course, this will happen once Google knows that your content actually exists. However, once it does know that your content exists, Google records the date that it found that content in its indexes.

When you browse the Web have you ever noticed that some of the top listings are for articles that have been published years ago? This is because the content has become well aged. Not only did the content have all the other right factors for SEO, but also years had passed since that content was first found by Google, and Google trusts that content because it's been around for a very long time.

Now, you may be thinking, how are you supposed to build content that's aged right away? Well, you can't unfortunately, however, you can start right now by beginning to create content that Google will index and find.

PINGING YOUR CONTENT

When you create content, it's important to ping that content. When you ping a piece of content, it tells Google's spiders to go forward and index that page. Otherwise, you can't ever determine just when Google will visit and index your page. However, when it's pinged through a service like Pingler.com or Linklicious.me, you'll know that Google has gone to index that page.

Once you've pinged the content, it begins the countdown to begin aging. All you need to do in order to ping the content is logon to any of the online Web pinging sites such as Pingler.com and enter in the URL. Pingler.com is a free service, but also offers a paid service that automatically pings on a schedule that you assign it (anywhere from 3 to 10 days).

Without pinging a link you cannot start the countdown

to begin aging the content. This is something that you need to get into the habit of doing as soon as you release a piece of content out there onto the Web. You always have to ping it with one of the online pinging services.

3
BUILDING TRUST THROUGH AUTHORITY

Since Google's trust needs to be earned nowadays, the best way for you to earn that trust is by getting other sites that Google already trusts to link to you. This is also known as building authority. You can build authority by using existing sites that already have high PageRanks.

This is something that you most likely already do every day for other Websites when you, for example, share a link to a news article through social media, or post a link to a photo from some Website that you found interesting. Every time you do this, you are helping to build authority for the domain name that contains the link.

When you begin building links back from authority Website's to your own site, you begin to build your own Webpage's authority. This is extremely simple and it's the first step that you should take to SEO your site.

To start out, simply logon to any of the sites in the proceeding list. If you already have an account, great, then you won't need to set one up. If you don't have an account, then set one up, and as soon as you do, create a link back to your own Website in your profile on that particular site.

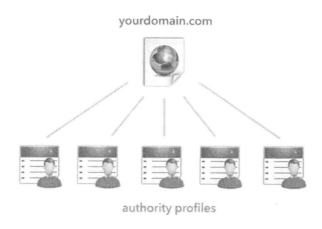

authority profiles

- Blinklist.com

- Delicious.com

- Diigo.com

- Deviantart.com

- Facebook.com

- Folkd.com

- Friendfeed.com

- Hi5.com

- Identi.ca

- Jumptags.com

- Kaboodle.com

- Karmalynx.com

- Kippt.com

- LinkedIn.com

- LinksaGoGo.com

- Livejournal.com

- MyAOL.com

- Myspace.com

- Netlog.com

- Newsvine.com

- Pheed.com

- Pintrest.com

- Plurk.com

- Plus.Google.com

- Reddit.com

- Scoop.it

- Serpd.com

- Skyrock.com

- Slashdot.com

- Sonico.com

- Springpad.com

- Stumbleupon.com

- Tagged.com

- Twitter.com

- Typepad.com

- Vk.com

- Webshare.com

- Xing.com

- Zootool.com

Now, the best approach to doing this is to actually split the list apart and do one or two profile each day, then ping Google and let it know where to go to index the profile page so that it can log the link that you've created in your favor. If you do them all at once, you still shouldn't have a problem, but the best fully organic approach is to split the list apart and do it little by little, informing Google by pinging it the URL each step of the way.

Beyond the Authority Profile Pages

Once you've tackled the profile page links, the next important step to building authority is by having other very high PageRank Websites, linking to you through unique content. This is going to require some work on your behalf, but these sites are incredibly popular authority sites that anyone can post content to.

Be prepared to begin blogging and writing unique, well-researched articles that are at least 500 words that contain links back to your Webpage. Both Webpages (the one on your Website and the one on the authority Website) should both have separate unique content about the same primary keyword.

For example, let's say your page is about bunny rabbit cages then you would create a unique article about bunny rabbit cages on your own Website. Afterwards, you would create another article about bunny rabbit cages (or a video, or slideshow presentation) on the authority Website. However, the article on the authority Website would link to the article on your Website using your primary keyword. This would build instant authority.

This method works extremely well when both pieces of content are highly optimized and I will discuss how to do this in the coming chapter. The proceeding image is a graphical representation of what this would look like. The arrow indicates that the link is traveling from the authority site to your Webpage.

Here is a list of the authority Websites that you can

begin creating content on immediately. You sh
course, also create links on your profile page on these
Websites as well. Aside from that, you can build content
on each of these very high PageRank Websites. YouTube
is the only site that you will be able to create video
presentations on but that is also one of the most effective
ways to begin building content.

- Squidoo.com

- Tumblr.com

- Slideshare.com

- HubPages.com

- Scribd.com

- YouTube.com

PROCEEDING WITH CAUTION

One important thing to note here is that when creating links from sites like authority sites, it's easy to go overboard. What does this mean? It's easy to go out there, get very excited about your site and start spamming a ton of links within moments of each other through all of the social media sites available. This is not a good thing.

It's okay to take one article or one piece of content from your site and share it across as many different platforms as possible. However, don't do this for multiple articles each day. As much as you think you will be helping your site, you may in fact be hindering it by over posting. This is something that the Google Penguin targeted and it's something that you need to be aware of.

Sometimes in the wake of these new Google SEO rules, you're going to feel like you're walking a bit of a tight rope because you are. You don't want to overdo it or you'll end up in the Sandbox and that's not where you want to be, especially if you already have an aged domain. Take it easy with the posting and allow it to happen naturally and organically. Post a few articles or content each week and share each of those as much as possible.

I will be discussing some techniques to use some syndication services that are available for sharing your content across different social media networks automatically in coming chapters. For now, just keep in mind that everything you do should be done as naturally and organically as possible to not rock the boat. This holds especially true if your site has no links to it when you start out.

Google keeps track of all of these things along with your link acceleration – or the pace at which the number of links that you have increases each month. Basically, Google keeps track of everything related to your site, all the time. It's like Big Brother watching over you now so be aware of that and always keep it in the back of your mind.

4
BUILDING TRUST THROUGH CONTENT

Trust through content is built by writing well-researched, unique articles that are optimized for On-Page SEO. On-Page SEO is anything that is done in SEO on your actual Webpage itself. Sometimes this is also referred to as On-Site SEO, but they both have the same inherent meaning.

Building trust through content is one of the easier parts of your SEO workload because you actually have full control over this. Unlike Off-Page SEO (link building and content building that happen away from your Website) you get to have full reign on completely optimizing your pages for SEO so take advantage of it.

The name of the game today, in the wake of Google's World Wide Web War is relevancy. You want to appear as relevant as possible to Google's search engine. To be considered relevant, you first need to have relevant content. Relevant content comes by fully optimizing your pages for your primary keyword.

We'll get into keyword research in the next chapter, but I first wanted to paint you a picture of how the process works so that you have an overview before you start diving in and getting your hands dirty.

Overall, you know now that there are three major components to building trust. This happens through: age, authority and content. Some of these components intermingle with one another. For example, when you're building trust through authority (backlinking) you have to have your content optimized first. All three work hand-in-hand and not one of these on their own, or even two will do it for you; you need all three in perfect order.

When it comes to your content, however, it's simply important to realize that it has to be excellent. Don't try to take any shortcuts here. Google is getting better and better at analyzing content for not only duplicity, but also uniqueness, and overall value as well. Their algorithms have been developed over the course of over 15 years now by some of the greatest minds on the planet. Simply put, you need to do the work now.

To give you a brief overview at first, when you build trust through content you are going to be doing the following three things:

1. Researching Keywords

2. Writing your Content

3. Optimizing your Content

The keyword research will help you to pinpoint your primary keyword. The primary keyword will be the target of your content writing and optimization efforts. When you know what keyword you're targeting, how many people are searching for that keyword, and how much competition there is, then you'll have a much better idea of how quickly you'll be able to rank high on Google's SERPs.

Since you're going to have much less control over the Off-Page SEO factors that affect your Website, it's important that you put as much time as possible into your On-Page SEO efforts. Building trust through content is important and I cannot stress enough how detail oriented you need to be in this stage of your SEO efforts.

Many people with their own Websites gloss over the content writing part. They quickly slap together text for articles and Website copy then they're left with a subpar product. That may have used to work a few years back, but after all of the algorithm changes, it doesn't anymore. Take the time and be detailed oriented in this stage because it will make the world of a difference for you in your overall rank.

OVER-OPTIMIZATION WARNING

With the release of the Google Panda & the Google Penguin, Google has become very particular with sites that are attempting to over-optimize their content. If your content does not sound natural and it looks like your keywords are too forced, you will not rise in the rankings, and risk being demoted for those particular search keywords.

When you are writing your content, keep it very natural sounding. You do not have to use your keyword in the exact search term in each section. You can do variations from time to time, which will in fact help you rank higher. This is called LSI, or Latent Semantic Indexing. LSI is a technology used by Google to determine similar words and phrasing for search terms, but don't beat yourself up trying to force your keyword term in each area. Keep it as natural sounding as possible for the best results.

5
ON THE HUNT FOR KEYWORDS

Keyword research is at the core of content creation geared towards SEO. Selecting and finding the right keyword is the first step in creating content that will rank for that keyword. I've done a lot of keyword research in my life and through that experience I've learned to be able to know what to look for when conducting the research.

The first thing to keep in mind is that, in the beginning, the shorter the keyword, the harder it will be for you to rank, especially if you haven't created trust through age yet. Here's an example:

1. Stop smoking (short keyword)

2. How to stop smoking cigarettes (long-tail keyword)

3. How to stop smoking cigarettes fast (long-tail

keyword)

The first keyword, stop smoking, is a short keyword. A keyword like this will have a lot of competition and even for an established Website with a lot of age and authority, it will be difficult to rank in the top spot. For that reason, you should start out with long-tail keywords, keyword phrases with 4 or more words in them.

A long-tail keyword should be your target in the beginning, especially if you're starting out with a new Website and new domain name. Why? Long tail keywords have less competition and are far easier to rank at the top of Google's SERPs. Even if you have a brand new Website, as long as you build some good authority and have excellent optimized content, you have a chance of ranking in the top few spots for low competition keywords.

Wouldn't you rather rank high on a SERP with few searches every month than virtually not be found in the depths of SERPs for higher searched keywords? Each time, hands down, it's better to rank high on a keyword with few searches each month than rank very low on a keyword with lots of searches each month.

FINDING THE RIGHT LONG-TAIL KEYWORDS

First introduced back in August of 2008, the Google autosuggest feature is something that you probably already use every day. To use this, just navigate to a Google search page for your country and begin typing in a keyword. As you type in the keyword you'll notice a drop-down box with some suggestions. This is how you'll find your primary keyword, by using Google's autosuggestions.

Let's extend our cigarette smoking example and begin with the keyword "how to stop smoking cigarettes." When you type that in and then hit the spacebar you'll notice many different variations of the phrase are suggested. Most of these are usable options but they will need to be able to apply to what your page's content will be about so sort through the list carefully.

As you run through this list, jot down all of the suggestions for keywords that you think you may want to use to target the content of your Webpage for. Here are the suggestions provided by Google for that search:

1. How to stop smoking cigarettes during pregnancy

2. How to stop smoking cigarettes yahoo answers

3. How to stop smoking cigarettes without medication

4. How to stop smoking cigarettes fast

5. How to stop smoking cigarettes cold turkey

6. How to stop smoking cigarettes naturally

7. How to stop smoking cigarettes and weed

8. How to stop smoking cigarettes while drinking

9. How to stop smoking cigarettes without gaining weight

10. How to stop smoking cigarettes and not gain weight

Google

```
how to stop smoking cigarettes
how to stop smoking cigarettes during pregnancy
how to stop smoking cigarettes yahoo answers
how to stop smoking cigarettes without medication
how to stop smoking cigarettes fast
how to stop smoking cigarettes cold turkey
how to stop smoking cigarettes naturally
how to stop smoking cigarettes and weed
how to stop smoking cigarettes while drinking
how to stop smoking cigarettes without gaining weight
how to stop smoking cigarettes and not gain weight
```

Google is making these suggestions to you based on what everyone is searching for using its search engine. One important thing to note is that on this list, the order that the search keywords are listed does not indicate the frequency of the searches or level of competition for the keywords. In order to determine how many searches each of the keywords receives, and the level of competition for each one, you'll need to use the Google Keyword Tool.

GOOGLE KEYWORD TOOL

You should take 3 to 5 of the most suitable keywords that you find in the autosuggestion drop-down list on the Google search and head over to Google's own keyword tool. You can find it by doing a Google search for "keyword tool" and it will be the first listing to appear in the search results. You can also head to the following link: https://adwords.google.com/o/KeywordTool

In the proceeding image you'll see the Google Keyword Tool Webpage. In it, I've entered in the 10 keyword suggestions provided by Google into the search box then conducted the search. I was logged into my Google account to do this, however, you don't need to be logged into your own to conduct the search. Even if you don't' have a Google account you can use the Keyword Tool, however, it becomes a nuisance after a while of having to enter in Captcha codes, but still you don't need a

Google account.

In the results, I get a list of the keywords that I've entered along with a few key detailed fields. Google tells me how many times the keyword is searched locally (based on your IP address), globally around the world, and how much competition there is. If you have a new Website, you cannot go after high competition keywords. Simply put, you just won't be able to rank well on these.

Of course, if you have some incredible circumstances such as a major mention from a high PageRank Website such as a site like Mashable.com or one of the other very popular news sites or blogs that would create some instant authority, you won't have the SEO juice to get ranked.

In the list, my original keyword of "how to stop smoking cigarettes fast" would be the best bet from the keywords entered. It has medium competition with low searches. Of course there is the keyword "how to stop smoking cigarettes and weed," that would be even better to target but you would need to assess if you wanted to write an article that targeted that keyword in the first place.

For all intensive purposes I'll assume you want to get ranked for the "how to stop smoking cigarettes fast" keyword. However, when you click on the "keyword ideas" tab you will get several other suggestions for long-tail keywords. One that seems very attractive is the "how to stop smoking and not gain weight" keyword, which has low competition and a fairly decent amount of searches. You could go after this keyword as well.

Can you see now how you can go about finding the right keywords to target? Your ultimate goal is to find keywords that have low competition and high search volume, but that doesn't paint the entire picture. Yes, we've been able to narrow down some keywords using both the Google Autosuggestion and the Google Keyword Tool but your work is not done there.

USING SEO QUAKE

The final ingredient to the keyword puzzle is a tool called SEO Quake. I spoke about this tool in my other book entitled *The SEO Black Book – A Guide to the Industry's Secrets*, and I still believe strongly in this tool. The reason why SEO Quake is such a great tool is because it will allow you to put on x-ray glasses to see through the Google search results to find some very hidden important information.

Basically, SEO Quake is an extension or plug-in that you download and install for your browser. Currently, it's not available for Safari browsers on Macs but it does work for Firefox and Google Chrome. I personally use it with Google Chrome but you can also use it with Firefox and produce the same results. To install SEO Quake just search Google for the keyword "SEOQuake Chrome Extension" and install it as an extension to the browser.

only enable the Google search engine
ou're not slammed with a bunch of
nation for other less important search

nduct a search with SEO Quake installed,
you get a ..... bar of data underneath each listing that
highlights some important information. The information
that's in the bar addresses two main components of trust
for rankings and that includes the age and authority of the
content that's ranked in Google's search.

SEO Quake tells you the following:

1. Trust through content

    a. The PageRank of the Webpage

2. Trust through age

    a. Link to the WHOIS information for when
    the domain was registered online.

3. Trust through authority

    a. How many links the domain name has
    pointing to it

    b. How many links the Webpage has pointing
    to it

    c. How many Facebook likes it has

    d. How many Tweets it has

    e. How many Google Plus Ones it has

SEO Quake will mainly tell you information as it relates to the Off-Page SEO statistics of the Website, which is very important knowledge to help you come to a final determination of whether or not you will be able to rank your content at the top of a search. Although the PageRank number that's provided will also help you to determine just how popular that piece of content is, it's not a complete tell all for how well the specific page is optimized for On-Page SEO.

By looking at the top listings and when their domains were registered, that will be the first biggest indication of what your potential to rank at the top of the list will be. The other, authority factors, also come into play but the age will be the most important thing to look at.

Okay, let's take a look at a search with our example. Let's conduct a Google search for the following two keywords with the SEO Quake extension installed on Google Chrome:

1. How to stop smoking cigarettes fast

2. How to stop smoking and not gain weight

"How to stop smoking cigarettes fast" – Search Analysis

The red arrow indicates the SEO Quake toolbar in the proceeding image. This search has 110 global worldwide searches done each month with medium competition. When you step back to analyze that you may realize to yourself that it's not worth going after this keyword. Why?

Medium competition will be much harder to target than the low competition. Unless you have already built some authority, you should probably try to target a low competition keyword. But, you will need to make this decision on your own depending on your domain's age, authority and content (which we'll discuss in the proceeding chapters).

In the search for "how to stop smoking cigarettes fast," you'll see the top listing has a lot of links to its domain, and in fact it's over 123,000 links going to the domain (indicated by the "LD" symbol). Since this is the Reader's Digest Website this makes sense, but the page itself has no links going to it (indicated by the "L" symbol).

That could be a good indication that although the domain has a lot of links to other pages of its Website, if you were to out link the Reader's Digest Webpage to your specific page of content that competed on this search, on a slightly aged domain, you may have a chance for the number one spot. In order to make that determination, you have to look at the other factors involved along with the subsequent listings on this particular SERP.

In addition to the massive amounts of links to the Reader's Digest domain on the first listing, it also has an enormous number of Tweets and Facebook Likes. These are important because these are very high PageRank links and Google has been paying more and more attention to these as of recently.

On further analysis of this search, however, when you begin to look into the ages of each of the domain names by clicking the WHOIS links on the small tool bars it will launch a screen for you telling you when the domain name was registered. This would more or less provide you with the domain's age.

When we take a look at this particular domain's WHOIS record, we come to find out that it was registered in 1995. The second listing in this search result was registered in 1997, the third in 1999, and the fourth in 2004. This alone is a clear indication that this will be a very difficult search to rank a new domain name, even if it were a few years old since the top 4 spots were registered on or before 2004. This all indicates that it will be very difficult to get in one of the top few spots for this search even though it is a long-tail keyword.

In addition, it's important to note the PageRank of each listing. On the search that we just looked at for "how to stop smoking cigarettes fast," the top 3 listings have very high PageRanks of 4 and 5 (indicated by the "PR" symbol at the far left of the SEO Quake Toolbar). However, if you look at the 4th listing in the search, you will notice that is has no PageRank. So, how did this person get their content to the 4th position of this search?

Well, first of all the domain name is aged. It was first registered in 2004 (you can check this by clicking the WHOIS link on the SEO Quake toolbar beneath this listing). Secondly, you'll notice that it has a subdomain that features the partial search keywords of "stop-smoking". The hyphen makes no difference since Google disregards these special characters in its searches and results.

Now, on an even further analysis of the 4th listing, you'll remember that I discussed with you something called EMDs, or exact-match domains. Of course, this is not an exact match domain, but this Website owner was clever enough to create a subdomain with the keywords that he is targeting. As long as he has good content on his site, and it is not considered to be low quality the keywords in his subdomain actually help him rather than hinder him.

When you do click on the link to analyze the content,

this individual has spent an excruciating amount of time creating the content and crafting it to be very well optimized for Google's search engine. Since the base domain name was registered in 2004, and the content is excellent from an SEO standpoint, he was able to rank at the top of a medium competition search. Can you see how the analysis of this search using SEO Quake was helpful?

"How to stop smoking and not gain weight" – Search Analysis

Let's turn to the second contending long-tail keyword that we're analyzing in this example and take a look and see what types of results we get when we check "how to stop smoking and not gain weight." This was the "low" competition keyword if you'll remember, of the two.

The most important difference that you'll notice in this search term is that the PageRanks are much lower than in the first search. You see PageRanks of 2 and 3 in the top positions instead of 4 and 5. This is an enormous difference in PageRank, which exponentially increases as the numbers go up.

In the proceeding image, you'll see a graphical representation of PageRank, created by Elliance Inc., with some examples of sites that meet each PageRank. You'll notice in the graphic how Google is at the top of a very large mountain.

Not many sites fall between Google (PageRank 10) and GE.com (PageRank 7) and as you can see, a PageRank of 3 to 4 then to 5 are significant increases. The amount of traffic required to increase by just one PageRank at this level is exponentially greater than the level just below it. This makes an incredible difference in your ability to compete for certain keywords. As soon as the PageRank falls to a more manageable level it becomes much easier, such as in this second search with low competition.

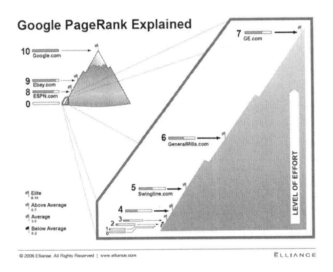

However, aside from the lower PageRank numbers in the top positions, if you conduct a WHOIS on the first position you will come to the realization that this Website was first registered in 2011.

When you take all the indicators of a low competition search, the first result is a relatively new domain name, and the top few results have low PageRanks, you quickly come to the realization that you will be able to compete much easier on this search keyword than on the first one.

PICKING A PRIMARY KEYWORD

When you've completed your analysis, select a primary keyword that you will use for your Webpage or blog article. Make sure that you've spent the time analyzing keywords using this method discussed before finding the right one to pick. If you're trying to write about a certain topic, look at it in different ways and ask questions. Use who, what, when, where and why question types to see what comes up in Google's autosuggestions.

You want to be sure you will be able to compete for the keyword so try to select one with low competition if at all possible, unless you already have an established Website or blog. If you do, then go for the medium competition keywords if you have to, but you'll find it much easier to get to the top of low competition searches in the beginning so try to stick with that.

6

WRITING & OPTIMIZING YOUR CONTENT

The Google search engine today is highly sophisticated. It has specifically designed algorithms that cannot only identify when content is written poorly, it can identify just how poorly that content has been written. As you know, Google is a pioneer in things like online language translations. It has created algorithms that analyze existing text within the context of its respective languages to identify patterns and specific phrases, even when they go against a standard set of rules for a direct translation.

Just as Google has done in pioneering translations, it has pioneered specific algorithms to determine how well your content sounds. It analyzes the types of words used, how they are used, and how frequently they are used. What all this means is that you need to pay very special attention to the content that you put out onto the Web; very special attention.

SEO WHITE BOOK – THE ORGANIC GUIDE TO GOOGLE SEARCH ENGINE OPTIMIZATION

When you write your content for your Webpage or article here is what you need to ensure that you do in order to meet the baseline specifications for good optimized content:

1. Select one primary keyword for your content

2. Write a 500-word minimum (1000-words recommended), unique, well-researched article or piece of Webpage content that adheres to the following set of rules:

    a. Has the primary keyword in the Webpage or article's title

    b. Has the primary keyword in the Webpage or article's meta description field

    c. Has a primary keyword density of 2% to 5% - meaning the primary keyword appears at least 2 to 5 times for every 100 words of content. For a 500-word article, the primary keyword should appear at least 10 times. However, the primary keyword must be used in the most natural sounding way and placed only within the flow of text. Otherwise, it can be considered keyword stuffing, a technique, when used, will see you drop in ranking.

    d. Uses the primary keyword at least once in the first paragraph and last paragraph of the Webpage

    e. Uses the primary keyword in the H1 (Heading 1) tag – this tag can be selected by highlighting the text and picking the Heading 1 style from the drop-down menu in a system like Wordpress.

f. Uses the primary keyword in the H2 (Heading 2) tag – this tag can be selected by highlighting the text and picking the Heading 2 style from the drop-down menu in a system like Wordpress.

g. Uses the primary keyword in the H3 (Heading 3) tag – this tag can be selected by highlighting the text and picking the Heading 3 style from the drop-down menu in a system like Wordpress.

h. Use your primary keyword once in bold font

i. Use your primary keyword once in italic font

j. Use your primary keyword once in underlined font

k. Use your primary keyword once in the image ALT tag attribute

3. Ensure that your Webpage title includes your primary keyword in the name of the page – if you use Wordpress you can do this by turning on permalinks with the "postname" option.

4. Any links to external pages must have the "nofollow" attribute, which tells search engines not to leave your page to go and index the page referenced by the link.

5. Create at least one internal link from within the

content of your Webpage or article to another page or article on your domain.

6. Create at least one external link to another Webpage on the Internet that uses your primary keyword with the "Nofollow" attribute.

On-Page Optimization

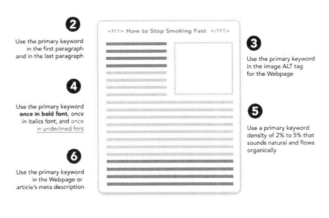

As you can see by the graphical representation of the Webpage, the primary keyword is everywhere, and this is what indicates to Google that your page is relevant and optimized for that particular keyword. If you're using a system like Wordpress and want to modify the meta description field for each page or article that you post, you need to have a plugin installed. I would recommend the Wordpress SEO plugin by Yoast. It's an excellent way to modify the meta description on each piece of content you put online.

Additionally, if you're using Wordpress, make sure that you enable the permalinks in the Wordpress options and set the option to "postname". This will then take the page title with your primary keyword and make it into the name of the page.

Please note, however, if you're switching from non-permalinks to permalinks while you already have content on your Wordpress site, you may experience issues so make sure you do a backup before you do this.

USING LSI IN YOUR CONTENT

If you're just hearing about Latent Semantic Indexing (LSI) here then it's something important that you need to pay attention to. LSI can be an excellent way to use your keyword many more times without it seeming like you're engaging in keyword stuffing. The mathematics behind LSI can get fairly complex but the general notion is that Google has been placing a heavier weight on word relationships as opposed to specifically matching exact keyword strings.

How does this impact you? Well, for one thing, this makes your job of writing your content significantly easier. Instead of trying to force, in our example, the keyword "how to stop smoking and not gain weight," you could substitute (as some of the listings do on the results page for that search) the word "stop" for "quit", "and not" for "without", and also use the variant "gain" by saying "how to quit smoking without gaining weight".

Google uses mathematics and several other correlations from existing information it has stored in its databases to determine that these are the same phrases. So, let's just say you have a 500-word article for "how to stop smoking and not gain weight," you could do all variations of that a few times to reach your 2% to 5% keyword density. You could use:

- Quit smoking without gaining weight

- Don't gain weight after your quit smoking

- Avoid weight gain after you stop smoking

- Stopping smoking and not gaining weight

- Stop smoking without weight gain

As you can see there are many different variants of the same keyword phrase. Try not to vary them too wildly, but just stick with a few different variants and use them like that. As you can see in our example for the search term "how to stop smoking and not gain weight," none of the top listings had that exist term but they all meant that exact same thing. Does this make sense?

Google most likely is also focusing heavily on this due to an old practice of keyword stuffing, and its efforts to avoid Websites who try to forcibly use the same keyword over and over in the page content too many times making it sound unnatural.

You can use LSI to make your page content sound

much more natural and it will be easier to write. When you stylize your text within your page you can pick and choose what variant of your keyword to style because Google will recognize it either way. It will know what your page is about by using its mathematical computations. It's your job, however, to ensure that you use still hit those rules for On-Page SEO discussed no matter how much LSI is used.

WORDPRESS PLUGINS

If you're using Wordpress for your Website, along with the 60 million other people who are, I would highly recommend installing a plugin for SEO to make your job easier. Why? Plugins for SEO help you easily keep track of things like your SEO Score. In my other books I always recommend the Yoast Wordpress SEO plugin but there are a lot very good plugins that you can use.

SEOPressor is another excellent Wordpress SEO plugin as well, however, that one is not free. The one thing that I really like about the SEOPressor plugin is that it has an LSI engine built into it (although it's Microsoft Bing's LSI). You can find SEOPressor by following this affiliate link here: http://bit.ly/seopressorv5 or you can simply Google "seopressor" and find it that way. Do some research into it and see if it's right for you.

7

LINKING TO YOUR CONTENT

One of the most important, and arduous, efforts for a search engine marketer (SEM) is engaging in link building for your content. This takes concerted time and effort that some people simply don't have. If you're doing SEO as a profession then that is one thing, however, for most people who are simply trying to optimize their own sites, these tasks can be daunting.

So, in order to not get overwhelmed, what I usually like to recommend is to break the link building tasks down into an hour or two each day. Just set that time aside and know that this is what you will be doing during that hour or two. In *The SEO Black Book - A Guide to the Industry's Secrets* I discuss using some different services to automate the link building. But, it's important to note that if you go down that route you may risk flagging with Google depending on what link building service you use.

For example, what Google has been doing recently is

finding links that look unnatural on blogs and forums and so on, and flagging those links as "link schemes", thus penalizing the site the link is directing to. Now, if you're going to take a fully White Hat SEO approach, you should not engage in this type of link building.

Instead, all of your link building should be natural and organic link building. This comes from placing links in blog comments and forum posts on the most part. Conduct a search on the Web and look for blogs and forums that are popular in your niche or industry. You'll want to target as many high PageRank forums and blogs as you possibly can (download the toolbar from alexa.com to determine PageRank).

Some forums will only allow you to post links (usually in your signature) after a certain number of days after signing up or after a certain number of posts. Each forum that you post on has its own set of rules regarding spamming and the sharing of links. Read the rules and get to know the forum and take the time to read posts and effectively communicate with the members in those communities.

If you keep in mind that your forum posts and blog comments should always provide some value and not be considered spamming, then this approach will work great for boosting your link visibility, but it requires a real concerted effort on a consistent basis.

What's most important to remember when building your links to your own content is that you build links back from sites that matter. Try not to go posting on blogs or forums with low PageRanks too much. While it's good to have some links from lower PageRank sites, spending a lot of time building links from very low PageRank blogs and forums probably will not be worth your while.

High PageRank Links

As I mentioned earlier, at the start of this book, it's imperative that you have high PageRank backlinks to your Website. One way to start out by doing this is by adding your Website link into the profile page of the following Websites. By doing this, you are creating some very important link relationships in the mind of Google's search engine algorithm. This is a critical step to starting out so ensure that this is done.

- Blinklist.com

- Delicious.com

- Diigo.com

- Deviantart.com

- Facebook.com

- Folkd.com

- Friendfeed.com

- Hi5.com

- Identi.ca

- Jumptags.com

- Kaboodle.com

- Karmalynx.com

- Kippt.com

- LinkedIn.com

- LinksaGoGo.com

- Livejournal.com

- MyAOL.com

- Myspace.com

- Netlog.com

- Newsvine.com

- Pheed.com

- Pintrest.com

- Plurk.com

- Plus.Google.com

- Reddit.com

- Scoop.it

- Serpd.com

- Skyrock.com

- Slashdot.com

- Sonico.com

- Springpad.com

- Stumbleupon.com

- Tagged.com

- Twitter.com

- Typepad.com

- Vk.com

- Webshare.com

- Xing.com

- Zootool.com

One thing to note about Facebook is that if you have privacy filters in place, Google will not be able to index your Website link from your personal profile. If that's the case, create a business page for your Website and place the link there and get Google to index that page. How is that done? Simple, by doing something called "pinging" your content to Google.

PINGING YOUR CONTENT

When you ping your content you tell Google to go to that page and index that information. A great place to ping your content is through Linklicious.me, a Website that offers a free pinging service of up to 2,500 links per day (more than you will ever need when engaged in a fully White-Hat SEO approach).

Pingler.com also offers a free pinging service, but more importantly it offers a service that will allow you to tell Google to come back every few days based upon whatever schedule you setup. This, however, is a paid service. I like to use Pingler on content that I know I want Google to come back to and keep re-indexing so that it's fresh in its database. It's up to you whether you want to do the same.

Every time you place a link to your site, anywhere, copy that link and ping it through one of these services or any other service online that offers pinging. This is an important concept to understand and something that you should get very used to doing. Once it's pinged, Google will go to that site and index the information for calculation into its search indexes. If you don't ping the link, then you won't be sure when Google will actually visit it. Get in the habit of pinging your links anytime you create any content on the Web that has a link to your site.

BUILDING CONTENT ON AUTHORITY WEBSITES

Leveraging existing authority Websites to build content that then links back to your Webpage is an excellent way to earn Google's trust. Here's how this process works:

1. Identify the type of content that you will post such as a video, article or slideshow presentation and select the site to post it to.

2. Optimize the content that you create on the authority site (or the content's description in the case of YouTube videos).

3. Link the content back to your optimized content with the same keyword (or an LSI variation) that

houses the destination content.

Why is this important? It's because Google already trusts these Websites and if you can harness the power of these sites to post content that ranks high, then get that content linking back to your own site, you could be on your way to exiting that Sandbox much more quickly in the case of a new Website.

You can utilize the following authority Websites to both post content and link back to your own Website. Each site has its own set of rules with regards to this and some are stricter than others. However, all of these sites offer very high PageRank backlinks that, when combined with unique content, can offer a tremendous boost to your Website's visibility on Google's SERPs.

Squidoo.com – You can post blog articles on this Website but you are limited to placing links only in the suggested links area and you cannot post links throughout the article itself. It's important to be careful not to violate their Terms of Service (ToS) by posting spammy content or content that is specifically intended as advertisements. If you engage in this, you'll see your content removed very quickly.

Tumblr.com – An excellent resource to post just about anything and have it rank well if it's optimized correctly. You can post links, text, quotes, audio and video here. A lot of professional SEOs leverage Tumblr.com for their SEO work.

Slideshare.com – An extremely popular Website that was recently acquired by LinkedIn, with a very high PageRank that can be used to take your presentations viral. You can upload Word documents or PowerPoint presentations only. But, these documents will have tremendous visibility on Google's search engine. This is another site that you have to be extremely careful not to violate their Terms of Service (ToS) otherwise you will see your content be removed. Do not post spam or content that is advertising in any way. Simply post content that will engage, educate and provide value to readers with a link back with your primary keyword to the same content on your site.

HubPages.com – This site is a lot more flexible when it comes to blogging and has more of a Wordpress feel in terms of being able to add links throughout the article that you post. HubPages.com is also a high PageRank Website and if you optimize the content properly with a link back to your site, this will give you a huge boost in terms of SEO value in the eyes of Google.

Scribd.com – Another site like HubPages.com, and also with a very high PageRank. Use Scribd.com to post articles, PDF files, Word documents, PowerPoint presentations and so on. All of these files will get indexed by Google once you ping it to visit so make sure that you follow along with the optimization tips for writing the articles. The best program to use is Microsoft Word where you can indicate heading tags and other HTML within the document that will get translated when Google crawls the content.

YouTube.com – There's not enough that can be said about YouTube. Google loves YouTube videos, especially ones that provide value. When you shoot a YouTube video, make it informative and engaging. Try not to be dull and boring so that you can get people to like your video and share it with others. Embed your video into your articles or Webpages that target the same content or keyword. In addition, provide some transcription information into the description of the YouTube video, which works really well for SEO purposes. YouTube videos get ranked very high so if you want to target a keyword search shoot a YouTube video and optimize it then ping it to rank.

Building authority content can be a lot of work and it can get overwhelming, but if you limit yourself to doing this a little bit each day and possibly building one good piece of content every day or every other day and optimizing that content, in no time you will have created incredible SEO juice for your site.

Each of the pieces of content that you create on these authority Websites will rank themselves, especially YouTube videos. YouTube itself is like a search engine and if you do searches on Google you will notice a lot of YouTube links come up at the top. Use this to your advantage. If you have a new Website this is probably the single best resource to begin promoting your Website and driving traffic.

Content Marketing

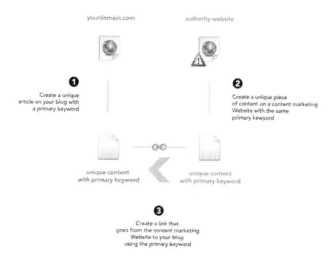

The preceding image illustrates an overview of how the process of creating content on an authority Website that then links back to your own content, works. For maximum efficiency the unique authority content that you create should link to your own content that is also unique.

Both pieces of content should be optimized for the same primary keyword. However, the inbound link should be from the authority Website to your own using the primary keyword. This will create a boost in search engine visibility by providing a high PageRank back link from unique content on an authority site, and give you the SEO boost that you need no matter if your site is new or old.

You should take this approach by creating different content on all the authority Websites then linking back all to other unique content on your own site. As you can imagine, this takes a lot of work but this will provide the single biggest SEO value for your domain.

8
SOCIAL MEDIA STRATEGIES

Social factors influence the rank of your Website and that of your content. Remember the example of the searches conducted with SEO Quake? Well, one way for a listing to move ahead of others with equal PageRank is through high social rankings with likes from Facebook, tweets from Twitter, and plus ones from Google Plus.

It may be overwhelming to think about everything that needs to be done to create, optimize and distribute your content, but once you've done it a few times successfully, you will quickly get the hang of it. Here's an overview of the process thus far:

1. Create the content

2. Optimize the content

3. Distribute the content

When you distribute the content you do that through Off-Page SEO link building. This can happen through any of the channels that I've discussed thus far, but the most important primary channels that exist are through social media. However, leveraging social media has itself turned into an art form. People are very turned off when they see blatant advertisements in social media, so you have to resort to more clever social media strategies if you want to get those links to your Website to start spreading throughout the Internet.

LINK BAIT STRATEGY

Ever login to Facebook and see some ingenious photo with a quote on it that makes you laugh, cry, sing or anything in between? Sure you have, everyone has. And when you see this photo, doesn't it make you want to be the first one to share it with all of your friends? Of course it does because it does for nearly everyone, that's why it's such a successful strategy. This is what you call link bait.

Link bait is a link to something created for the sole purpose of getting people to like it and share it. It is a very clever and unique method of building backlinks. Now, there are the people that do this simply for entertainment purposes because they have some great skills in a design program like Photoshop, but most of the time, the creation of link bait is done with the sole purpose of generating back links.

If those back links go to a profile that then goes to a Website, then this is also in essence creating links back to your site that become more powerful. This is almost like creating what's called a link pyramid. When a social media profile is very strong (i.e. lots of friends, shares, connections, etc.) then the link back to the site it has in its profile becomes much more prominent. Google takes all of this into account.

This link bait creation can be done in the form of images, videos, and just about any other format that's shareable on the Web. When it's a video and it becomes viral, this is probably the strongest type of link bait that can exist. A viral video with millions of hits linking to a particular Website is an enormous booster for that site's visibility on Google.

However, creating link bait is easier said than done. You have to be a professional graphic designer, or have a very ingenious idea for an image with a quote. But, if you spend the time on this and you are successful, you will get a much more positive response than if you were to try to spend your time on designing ads to post on social media. People don't like blatant ads especially for businesses or brands that are not household names.

CONTENT SYNDICATION

There's not enough that I can say about content syndication. This is probably one of the best methods for streamlining some of your SEO work. What is it? Well let's just say you have 10 different social media networks that you post updates on or link to your content for SEO purposes. Content syndication takes all of those social media networks and allows you to post through one single repository that spreads it through all of these without having to login to each one separately.

There are a lot of different content syndication platforms out there. The one that I particularly like and always recommend is called Onlywire. You can follow this affiliate link - http://bit.ly/onlywirelink - or you can just Google "Onlywire" to find it. Onlywire is a paid service that works extremely well by syndicating on up to 51 social networks.

Now, you may be thinking that you don't even have 51 social media networks that you're subscribed to but that's okay. You can select the ones you want to use from their configuration options, but personally, I use all of them because each one is a link boost for your site so harnessing all 51 at once is an incredible link juice booster.

CONTENT COLLABORATION

Content collaboration is when you work with other like-minded SEO and SEM specialists to market each other's content. How does this work? There are a few different Websites that are devoted to content collaboration. One of them that I personally use is called TribePro.

With TribePro, you syndicate, and have syndicated, your content by all the other members in your tribe. You can have up to 5000 shares from different people on a single post with TribePro, but it takes time to build up to that level. In order to get there you have to syndicate people and they syndicate you back but it's a process of building this up over time by posting and syndicating.

When you post something through TribePro, not only does it syndicate your content on your own social networks selected, but on every other person's as well.

This can drop thousands of high PageRank back links in just a few minutes back to your Website's content. This is extremely powerful stuff. However, like with anything, this should not be abused. Posting tons of links each day will be seen as spamming and won't have the same effect as if you post only a couple per day.

However, TribePro is a paid service and for some they don't want to engage in paid services in order to promote their site. If you're a professional SEO specialist then this is a great resource to use, however, if you're just dabbling then you'll need to weight the cost to benefits for yourself as to whether or not you want to use this.

There are, however, other free content collaboration services out there on the Web. One is called EmpireAvenue. The concept is the same, but on EmpireAvenue you are awarded a certain number of the Website's own currency called Eaves. You can use those Eaves to issue missions for people to collaborate your content, or you can invest it in other members.

The Eaves are fictional but you can purchase more when you run out or simply allow time to elapse to earn more from your investments. It's an interesting concept that some people really take to. The site is used by some of the top online marketers to leverage the usage of real people to help them accomplish missions such as voting for something that they're a part of, liking a YouTube video and so on.

9
NEXT STEPS

SEO can be confusing. It has a lot of different little elements that all work together to come to one single glorious knot. However, the most frustrating part of SEO for most people is the fact that Google doesn't tell you what you need to do to rank better. Sure, there are tools such as the Google Webmaster Tools, which, if you aren't using you certainly should. However, aside from that, you won't know your score in any given trust component, you just have to work off of an element of faith that what you're doing is going to make an impact in the long run.

To me, this is one of my major dissatisfactions with the SEO industry, however, if this misinformation didn't exist, and people knew exactly what they had to do to get to the top of Google's SERPs, it would cause a clutter and chaos unlike ever before. What Google has done, and its sole purpose with its search engine, is to create the most relevant search results that it possibly can. Just think about it, when you're searching for something, you want to be sure that the top listings are relevant to what you need right? Of course you do.

This misinformation and disinformation in the market causes a lot of frustration, especially for newcomers to the industry. My biggest suggestions to you are to keep at it with SEO and not give up because it takes a significant amount of time investment and input to see ranking improvements, especially if you don't have that precious trust built up with Google already. Also to see major improvements in what you're doing expect to give it about 60 to 90 days from after you do all your optimization work. Yes, 60 to 90 days. I know it's a long time.

Google purposefully doesn't allow listings to jump around that quickly because it doesn't want SEO and SEM specialists knowing just how much improvement the changes that they made have created. Of course there's that coupled with the fact that Google's search engine spiders have to go out and index the entire Web, which is very, very, very large. Once it's all indexed then it computes and re-ranks everything. This takes a lot of computing power and doesn't happen that often.

Google has two types of spiders that go out. There are the quick, shallow indexing spiders, and then there are the long-term deep-indexing spiders. The quick indexing spiders can go out every hour, every day or every week depending on how much it trusts a certain site. If you have a very popular blog, for example, expect Google to be visiting it on its own every day without you having to let it know to come to it by pinging your URLs.

The deep-indexing spiders for Google do their work every 2 to 3 months to re-index the entire Web. This deep-indexing is revealed when you see the major improvements to your SEO work that you performed some time ago, start to show up.

Tuck this knowledge in the back of your mind and keep up the work on building links, creating content, and syndicating your site's pages as much as possible. The more work you put in, the more it will pay off in the long run.

I wish you the best of luck with your SEO efforts, and hopefully this SEO book provided you with the information and insight into the industry to begin conducting effective SEO for your Website today.

OTHER BOOKS BY THIS AUTHOR

If you enjoyed this book on SEO, I would really appreciate it if you could take a few moments and share your thoughts by posting a review on Amazon. You can post a review by visiting the following link - http://www.amazon.com/dp/B00BUOPFHI

I put a lot of care into the books that I write and I hope that this care and sincerity come across in my writing because in the end I write to bring value to other people's lives. I hope that this book has brought some value to your life. I truly do.

Also, feel free to also take a look at some of the other books that I have available on Amazon. The following titles can also be found that I have authored:

SEO Simplified – Learn Search Engine Optimization Strategies and Principles for Beginners - http://www.amazon.com/dp/B00BN7PGEY

SEO Black Book – A Guide to the Search Engine Optimization Industry's Secrets - http://www.amazon.com/dp/B00B7GIVSE

How Not to Give Up – A Motivational & Inspirational Guide to Goal Setting and Achieving your Dreams - http://www.amazon.com/dp/B00BSB02KI

Kindle Self Publishing Gold – Unlocking the Secrets of How to Make Money Online with Kindle eBooks - http://www.amazon.com/dp/B00BQJB5QM

Kindle Marketing Ninja Guide – Killer Marketing Strategies for Kindle Book Marketing Success - http://www.amazon.com/dp/B00BLR40FC

I wish you all the best in your SEO educational pursuits.

All the Best,

R.L. Adams

APPENDIX
SEO TERMINOLOGY

Aged Domains – An aged domain is a domain that has been in indexed by Google at least two or more years ago and it's a critical component of any successful SEO campaign. Google penalizes new domain names, making it very difficult to rank any keywords at the #1 position or even on the first page of search results for that matter in the beginning. Purchasing or having an aged domain will be one of the critical factors in your success for ranking a site high for any given keyword.

ALT tags – Also known as alternative tags, these are the tags that appear within the HTML <img> tags that present the alternate data to the search engines to provide a description of what the image is. For optimal search engine rankings you should have at least one image ALT tag that correlates with your site or page's primary keyword.

Backlinking – Likely to be your biggest undertaking when it comes to SEO, backlinking is the effort involved with creating hyperlinks that link back to your Website.

Black-Hat SEO – Black-Hat SEO is a term used to describe a SEO tactics that are not compliant with Google's Webmaster Guidelines. Black-Hat SEO techniques are frowned upon by the search engine industry. Examples of Black-Hat SEO techniques are trying to hide keywords within HTML comment tags or trying to cloak pages.

Breadcrumb – A navigational aid used on Websites, breadcrumbs not only allow users to quickly jump through informational sections on the site, they also provide high SEO value by allowing the search engine spiders access to quickly navigate and spider through a site, indexing data faster and more efficiently.

Cloaking – This is a technique that delivers different content to the search engine spiders then it does to real human visitors. The cloaking technique is oftentimes used to mask the real content or change the real content of a page and make it appear differently to a search engine spider. This is considered a Black-Hat SEO technique and while it is sometimes used for legitimate purposes, it is oftentimes used to display pornographic material to real human visitors while only displaying non-pornographic material to a search engine spider.

CPC – Cost-per-click, or CPC, is a term used in online paid advertising to indicate click through percentages. The cost per click is calculated by diving the number of clicks with the total amount spent on the advertisement. For example, if you spent $100 on an ad and 200 clicks was received; the CPC would be $0.50 cents.

CSS – Cascading Style Sheets, also known as CSS, is a style sheet presentation markup language that is used to position elements, layouts, colors, fonts, images, and construct a Web page on the whole. While CSS is used primarily in styling HTML Web pages, it is also used to style XML and other documents.

Dofollow Links – Dofollow links are an attribute associated with an HTML hyperlink that tell a search engine to continue to link through to the site, disseminating some of the site's important link juice. These are very powerful types of links that work well when pointed to your site or to a link pyramid that leads to your site. When a search engine sees a Dofollow link they continue linking through to the site, passing part of the SEO link juice that would have been offered to that page had the link been a Nofollow link.

Duplicate Content – In the search engine world, content is king, but duplicate content is the court jester. Copying large chunks of content to your site is one of the biggest no-no's in the industry. The search engines will figure it out sooner or later and you will be demoted in the rankings. If you're going to do SEO right, make sure all the content is high-quality and unique content that's well researched.

Headings – HTML headings are blocks of code that are placed around certain words, styling and providing a certain level of prominence in the overall page structure. Heading tags range from <h1> through <h6>, however, in the modern SEO world the first three hold the most importance. Tags <h1> through <h3> should all contain the primary keyword spaced throughout the page with the <h1> and <h2> tags being above the Website fold.

Internal Link – Internal links are links from your page's content to another page or section on the same domain. Internal links are important when it comes to On-Site SEO.

Keyword – A keyword is a word or phrase that is used to optimize a Website or Webpage. Selecting keywords is one of the most important tasks in SEO work and selecting the right keywords in the outset can either make or break you. It's important to note that the keyword "Miami vacation" and "vacation Miami" will produce different search results, so the order and positioning of the words within the phrase is just as important.

Keyword Density – The keyword density is the number of times a keyword appears on a page in relation to the total number of words. Optimal keyword density ranges from 2% to 5% with anything considerably over 5% being construed as SPAM and anything considerably lower then 2% being construed as not keyword rich enough and thus less relevant. It's important when writing your content that your primary keyword is evenly distributed throughout the page, making sure that it appears in the first and last sentence of the content as well as evenly spaced throughout the balance of the words.

Keyword Stuffing – Keyword stuffing is the over usage of a keyword in content or meta keyword tags, something that used to be popular many years ago, but is now frowned upon as a Black-Hat SEO technique. Keyword stuffing is achieved in various different ways which include placing the phrase multiple times within the Meta tags while combined with other words in different combinations, applying the same color to the keywords as the background making them invisible, using the <noscript> tag, and using CSS z-positioning. All of these practices will get you demoted and sometimes de-indexed by search engines like Google.

Long Tail Keyword – A long tail keyword is a keyword that has a minimum of at least 3 words and any maximum number of words. Long tail keywords are used by marketers trying to target a specific niche, question or topic, which produce near similar results to a broader search term of lessor keywords but may have higher competition. Long tail keywords are a great way to rank at the top of search engine results for terms that may otherwise be more difficult to rank for.

Link Bait – Link Bait refers to content that is created in order to garner as many links to it as possible. Since backlinks are one of the primary drivers of SERP positioning, many SEO efforts include the creation of content with the primary goal to get as many links back to that content as possible.

Link Farm – A link farm is a group of sites that all hyperlink to one another, back and forth in an oscillating fashion. While link farms used to be advantageous, they don't have large relevancy today since the two-way links make it confusing for search engines to determine which site is the vendor and which is the promoting site.

Link Juice – This is the SEO linking power of a page and usually refers to the combined sum of the link power of all the pages linking into it. You'll hear the term link juice referenced when quantifying the power of a certain link or a page that those links lead to.

Link Pyramid – A Link Pyramid is a very powerful form of Off-Site SEO backlinking that involves the creation of a linking structure that is extremely powerful. Think of the strength in physical form that a real pyramid has and how the transference of force is physically supported by the structure itself and how that has stood the test of time. Link Pyramids generally have three tiers: a bottom tier with low level links, a middle with medium level links, and a top level with high level EDU, GOV or other authority links. The bottom links link to the middle, the middle links link to the top, and the top links link to your site.

Link Sculpting – When you implement attributes to links to affect their behavior in how search engines interpret them, you're engaging in link sculpting. The most common form of link sculpting is using the Nofollow or Dofollow link sculpting forms. The Nofollow links tell a search engine not to follow a link, thus leaving the link juice on the page, while a Dofollow link tells a search engine to continue on to follow that link thus disseminating the link juice to the next page.

Link Wheel – A Link Wheel is a form of linking that links one site to another while also linking back to your site as well. The links flow in a sort of wheel format with the spokes being links back to your site in the center. When done correctly, a link wheel can be a powerful form of SEO boost for your Website and the most effective forms of link wheels are organically fashioned ones that utilize social media platforms as their linking mediums.

Meta Keywords – Meta keywords are part of a set of Meta Tags that appear in the header of Websites. Meta keywords used to be prominently used in search engine rankings but have no interpreted value of importance today. Instead of using meta keywords, search algorithms now use other tags such as heading tags, site content, keyword density and backlinking keywords to determine search engine rankings.

Meta Description – The meta description tag is one of the meta tags that are still used by search engines to display search results. This along with the title tag is used to display the name and description of the link on SERPs to the user searching for information.

Nofollow Links – Search engines spider the Web looking for information and in turn ranking the relevance of sites in its indexes. Nofollow links are an HTML attribute associated with hyper links that tell a search engine to not follow the link, stopping the search engine's traffic at that page, almost like a dead end. Nofollow links are optimal when it comes to making sure that your own page is optimized to the highest level possible by not allowing the link juice to pass through it.

Off-Site SEO – Off-Site SEO are the methods and practices of performing SEO work that happen away from the site itself. Off-Site SEO mainly involves the use of heavy backlinking, social media shares, authority site content creation (i.e. squidoo.com, youtube.com, etc.), article spinning, and so on. Off-Site SEO is a very labor-intensive part of the SEO trade.

On-Site SEO – Any work that is done on the Website to increase the effectiveness of its SEO is considered On-Site SEO. This includes any HTML work, content creation, internal linking, setup, keyword distribution, and other related efforts.

Page Title – The HTML page title is the descriptive site title detail that resides within the page's <title> tags. This information is displayed by the search engines and is used in ranking the site on the SERPs. A good page title tag should be descriptive but not superfluous and should accomplish its goal in around 70 characters (the cut off point for most SERPs) with the use of the primary keyword.

Pinging – Pinging is a technique that notifies the search engines to go out and seek data from a URL. This is required because a lot of the link building that is done happens on low, or no page rank sites that do not get visited often or at all by the search engines. When a search engine is pinged to go out and index a URL you can be certain that the hyperlink to your site or to another link in a link pyramid that's pointing to your site, will be found and indexed.

Panda – The Google Panda is a change in the algorithm for Google's search results that was released in February of 2011. The effects of Panda were to demote low quality sites and promote sites with high quality well researched information. The effects of this release were widespread, making huge shifts in positioning on SERPs forcing some businesses to lose large volumes of search traffic while others were able to gain it.

Page Rank – One of the most important descriptors of a Web page, the page rank is a Web page's rank in relevancy on the Internet, ranging from 0 to 10. Sites like Facebook, Twitter, and Google's home page achieve Page ranks of 9 and 10, while lower trafficked sites have lesser page ranks.

Penguin – The Google Penguin was one of the latest major updates released to Google's algorithm on April 24th, 2012, that began to demote visibility of listings on

SERPs that violated Google's Webmaster guidelines and employed Black-Hat SEO tactics such as cloaking, keyword stuffing, and the creation of duplicate content.

PPC - Pay-per-click advertising, or PPC, is a form of paid search engine advertising that marketers use to get their message out to the masses on a large scale very quickly. PPC ads show up on the right side of SERPs and are now also being implemented on Facebook, YouTube videos, and more recently on sites like Twitter.

PPV – Pay per view ads, or PPV, is a type of advertising that is utilized by marketers to distribute ads to a user base that has expressly agreed to receive those ads. An example of this is free software downloads or online services such as Pandora that use PPV ads to display advertisements on a periodic basis while providing a free service.

Referrer String – Referrer strings are used in affiliate and Web marketing to pinpoint campaigns and where a lead or referral came from. This is important to some marketers running paid advertisements to be able to gauge the successes of their various efforts throughout the Web. Web programming dictates that after the Web page name, a question mark can indicate the start of any variables that may be appended to a URL, thus resulting in a Referrer String.

Robots.txt – This is a file that resides in the root directory of your Website, that provides instructions to search engines on any folders, or files that it shouldn't index.

Most people don't want search engines seeing all files on their sites such as administration files, or other files that contain sensitive information.

RSS Feed – A Rich Site Summary (RSS) feed is a standardized format that allows for the automatic update and syndication of content on sites that have frequent changes and entries such as blogs and other news sites. The RSS feed format provides a standard in formatting that allows ease of redistribution of either full or summarized data, metadata and publishing information.

Sandbox – Google Sandbox Effect is an effect that happens when a newly formed domain name's link juice is not fully weighted due to filtering from Google in order to prevent SPAMMERS from reaching the first page in SERPs by registering multiple domain names quickly and actively promoting them.

Search Algorithm – A formula devised by brilliant minds that weighs and takes multiple factors into account when reaching a determination for search result page ranking. The Google search algorithm combines many factors including the aged domain factor, Website link popularity, On-Site SEO elements, and Off-Site SEO elements. No one outside of Google knows the exact current algorithm and the total weight of each of the factors that are taken into account or precisely how they impact search results but there are very good guidelines available.

SEM – SEM is the business of search engine marketing, the industry that search engine optimization specialists fall under. SEM is used to refer to not only SEO efforts but also paid search engine marketing efforts as well.

SERP – Search Engine Ranking Pages, also known as SERPs, are the end listing results pages of queries to search engines. SERPs will generally include a title and brief description of each listing related to the keywords searched along with a link to that content. In SEO the goal is to dominate the first page of SERPs.

Sitemap – A sitemap is a page that's created to aid browsers in crawling a site. A sitemap provides a hierarchical link structure of pages on a Website that are accessible and permissible to be crawled.

Social Media – Social media is a term that refers to the types of sites that have increased in popularity in the past several years that base themselves on end user interactions in a social and collaborative format. Examples of such popular sites are Facebook, Google Plus, and Twitter.

Spider – A Spider is a Web-robot that's instructed to go out and crawl the Internet for data used for the purposes of Website indexing and rankings. Google has multiple spiders that it sends out, some that are dedicated to deep-indexing the Web, others for more periodic updates to Web content, and even others for algorithm adjustments such as the Google Panda and Google Penguin.

Website Fold – The Website fold is the section of the Website that is viewable to the natural eye prior to getting cut off by the browser and forcing a user to scroll. The Website fold will vary from screen resolution to screen resolution, however it's typically 600 to 850 pixels down from the top of the browser.

White-Hat SEO – White-Hat SEO techniques are those that follow the rules and standards of the SEO world and also adhere to Google's Webmaster Guidelines. White-Hat SEO techniques, while more time intensive, offer the largest long-term gains for your Website's ranking on SERPs. These techniques include quality content creation, proper On-Site SEO configuration, and organically looking Off-Site SEO linking.

Made in the USA
Lexington, KY
31 May 2014